Job Interview Success for Introverts

Secure the job you want and deserve

Bob McIntosh

Impackt Publishing
We Mean Business

Job Interview Success for Introverts

First published: August 2014

Production reference: 1280814

Published by Impackt Publishing Ltd.
Livery Place
35 Livery Street
Birmingham B3 2PB, UK.

ISBN 978-1-78300-072-2

www.Impacktpub.com

Credits

Author

Bob McIntosh

Copy Editors

Maria Gould

Faisal Siddiqui

Production Coordinator

Melwyn D'sa

Reviewers

Arslan Ali

Karen M. Caito, CPC, ELI-MP

Adrienne Tom, CRS, CPRW, CEIP

Project Coordinator

Venitha Cutinho

Cover Work

Melwyn D'sa

Acquisition Editor

Richard Gall

Proofreader

Paul Hindle

About the Author

Bob McIntosh, a proud introvert, is a career trainer who leads more than 15 job-search workshops at an urban career center. Bob is qualified in the Myers-Briggs Type Inventory and leads an engaging MBTI workshop, in which he encourages introverts to realize their strengths and apply them to their job search. In addition, Bob is well known in the community as a LinkedIn authority; he teaches LinkedIn for Business workshops at a local community college. Bob's greatest pleasure is helping people find rewarding careers in a competitive job market. Follow Bob on Twitter at http://www.twitter.com/bob_mcintosh_1 and LinkedIn at http://www.linkedin.com/in/bobmcintosh1.

I'd like to thank my wife, Donna McIntosh, and my three wonderful children, Miranda, Chloe, and Robert for their patience and constant mention of introversion.

About the Reviewers

Arslan Ali has more than 14 years of experience related to the IT industry and training institutions with 5 years of exclusive experience in teaching various disciplines and projects in an IT institution. He has worked in various roles including software engineering, software testing, training, and quality assurance. The major focus of his expertise lies in coordination, implementation, and testing of ERPs and customized applications. He is also a trainer for context-driven testing for various companies and individuals.

Arslan is currently working at Sidat Hyder Morshed Associates as a Senior Consultant – Information Solutions; but besides that, he is also an active founding member of TestersTestified (www.testerstestified.com) (@testtified), Outtabox! (www.outtabox.co) (@OuttaBoxPk), and OISOL – Open Integrated Solutions (www.oisol.com) as a training consultant for software testing and context-driven testing workshops.

You can follow him on Twitter at @arslan0644 and on LinkedIn at pk.linkedin.com/in/thegoodchanges/.

I would like to thank Impackt Publishing for this opportunity and my father for his reading habits which I successfully inherited in me!

Prior to becoming a professional coach, **Karen M. Caito** has had 25 years of expertise as a pharmaceutical sales representative. Being an introvert and building confidence is a journey. She was able to experience first-hand how to thrive in an extroverted world by using several "techniques" to increase her confidence level so that she could achieve her life goals and create her niche coaching brand, *Confidence Coach for Introverts*. What she does best is help the overwhelmed, exhausted professional to become calm and confident so that the best version of themselves gets center stage in their health, career, and relationships, so they can finally be who they really are. She can stimulate that change in her clients in 90 days. Karen is also an Energy Leadership Expert, helping her clients discover the four Big Energy Blocks holding them back from success and catapulting them into abundant confidence with the use of the Energy Leadership Assessment Tool. She holds a BS in Marketing and Communications from Rochester Institute of Technology and is a NYS Licensed Massage Therapist. Her pharmaceutical career includes companies such as Bristol-Myers Squibb, Procter & Gamble, Sanofi-Aventis, and Merck. Visit her website at www.caitocoaching.com.

Adrienne Tom is an award-winning resume strategist and interview coach in Calgary, Alberta, Canada, with a passion for guiding senior-level professionals through the discovery of what sets them apart. Collaborating together, Adrienne works closely with senior professionals to develop leading edge marketing tools that help them stand out and advance their careers.

In addition to over 10 years in the career industry, Adrienne is a Certified Professional Resume Writer (CPRW), Certified Employment Interview Professional (CEIP), Certified Resume Strategist (CRS), and a member in good standing with three national and international career associations.

As a testament to her expertise, Adrienne has been the recipient of several prestigious industry awards, including six Awards of Excellence for outstanding resumes and outstanding online profile development from Career Professionals of Canada, as well as an international TORI Award (Toast of the Resume Industry) from Career Directors International. Her work has also been published in two national resume and cover letter books.

To learn more about Adrienne's specialized offerings for senior-level professionals, managers, directors, executives, and aspiring leaders, contact her at Career Impressions: www.careerimpressions.ca or info@careerimpressions.ca.

Contents

Chapter 3: Some Difficult Questions You'll Face at the Interview   37

Preface

So, you're an introvert

I was in my mid 40's when I discovered my preference for introversion. Until then, I thought I was an extrovert, mainly because I could, and still can, talk with ease to complete strangers. Truth be told, I hoped that my preference was for extroversion, not introversion, simply because society favors extroverts in most aspects of life: school, work, social interaction, and the job search, to name a few. I doubted my acceptance and didn't speak proudly of my preference until I learned more about the Myers-Briggs Type Inventory.

Do you remember when you learned your preference for introversion? Were you in doubt like me? Did you have a sense of dread thinking of the stereotypes of introverts, such as shy, loner, standoffish, aloof, recluse, or rude? Furthermore, you may have believed that introverts couldn't make small talk or associate with important, outgoing people.

But if all of this were true, how were you capable of talking with complete strangers, even approaching them, or want to be with your peers and attend social gatherings? How was it that some of your friends accused you of talking too much? And how have you been able to rub elbows with authorities in your town or city, to make small talk with the best of them? You were behaving more like an extrovert, weren't you? No, you were behaving like an introvert, able to adapt to your setting, and doing all the things mentioned here was a result of your introversion.

Now being an introvert doesn't seem so bad, does it? In fact, being an introvert has its benefits. You are an intelligent conversationalist. You think before talking and, therefore, don't make as many faux pas as some of your extroverted friends and colleagues. You are an engaged listener who doesn't think about what you'll say next before totally hearing the other person out. Being alone doesn't upset you; rather, you enjoy going to the movies alone and eating alone. Your friends and family can't understand this. You love writing and do it well. There are many things about being an introvert that you appreciate, feel comfortable with, and wouldn't want to change.

There are truths, though, that set introverts apart from extroverts; truths that put introverts at a disadvantage in life and the job search, especially at the all-important interview. Some of the strengths introverts possess can be faults, particularly when it comes to verbal communications. Talking, small talk to be precise, is a challenge for introverts because they feel the need to think before speaking, whereas extroverts will speak before thinking. Because of their inclination to think before talking, introverts are often left out of conversations.

In the job search, talking is integral to one's success. You can't rightfully go to a networking event and an interview and expect *not* to talk in the manner people expect you to. In other words, there are unspoken rules about conversing at networking events and interviews. Organized networking events are attended by people who see them as an opportunity to sell themselves. Often there is small talk which leads to delivering an elevator pitch. If the two parties are interested in what the other is selling, the conversation can extend. Some networkers like to "work the room," which means meeting as many people as possible, collecting as many business cards as they can. This is considered a success for the extroverts.

Success for introverts at a networking event looks a little different. Small talk becomes more like "deep talk." Introverts are not interested in the competitive nature of networking events. One of the Myers-Briggs Type Indicator questions goes something like this:

"When you are with a group of people, would you usually rather, A: Join in the talk of the group—or—B: Talk individually with people you know well?"

Can you guess how the introvert would answer? The second answer speaks to how introverts prefer to talk, not their ability to converse. Yet, this isn't how networking events work. Networking events are friendlier to extroverts.

At the interview, which is this book's ultimate focus, talking is paramount to success. Answering questions to the satisfaction of the interviewer(s) means the difference between winning the job or…going home the loser. This is not what you want. You want to succeed with flying colors at the interview, to hear the interviewer(s) say, "We'd like to offer you the job." You'll only hear these words if you're prepared for the all-important interview. Being prepared is also what this book is about. (I'll give you a hint; introverts are strong in the preparation department, more so than their counterpart, the extrovert.) On face value, the interview may favor the extrovert; but don't give up the battle just yet.

Introverts have a good sense of the job search in general; but we know that what matters is getting to the interview. You'll have to rely on your ability to analyze the steps it takes to get there, including your strong written communication skills, that is, CVs, cover letters, approach letters, and LinkedIn profile—along with your exerted efforts to talk. Some would argue you need to behave more like an extrovert, or utilize your extroverted traits. But there are characteristics of the introvert that are endearing to employers. You will learn what these are.

If introverts are labeled as quiet, having few friends, and private, then how does that propel them to succeed in networking and interviews? The answer to this question is thorough effort. This is what we'll look at when explaining how introverts can succeed in winning the position, leaving some extroverts out of the picture.

What does it mean to be an introvert? As I was explaining to my daughter, whom I suspect of being an introvert, introversion and extroversion are preferences; neither being better than the other. What I didn't explain to her are the challenges she'll most likely face. As an introvert, I face challenges every day, especially those surrounding talking. Which is ironic, especially since my occupation as a workshop facilitator at an urban career center requires me to talk all day. I chose my occupation because I'm good at disseminating information in a way people understand, but it does take a toll on my energy. I adapt.

So, your ability to talk will be challenged, and it's up to you to adapt to challenging situations –networking events, telephone interviews, and face-to-face meetings.

In this book, you'll learn how to conduct the job search that gets you to the interview. You'll also learn about questions from hiring authorities that may be a challenge. For example, one that would be a challenge for me would be, "Give us an example of when working as part of a team had a positive impact on the company, and what you learned about your ability to be a team player." You see, introverts don't prefer being on a team; rather, they like to solve problems on their own or with one or two other people. Then there's brainstorming and open work environments. Oh boy.

Let's begin our journey to the interview.

What this book covers

Chapter 1, Before the Interview, will demonstrate and outline the ways in which you can utilize the skills and typical work styles of an introvert to most effectively search for a job that will work for you. You will learn how to build your personal brand and present yourself successfully to prospective employers.

Chapter 2, You've Landed the Interview , Now What?, will talk about the best ways to prepare yourself once you have been invited to an interview. From researching the company and acquainting yourself with the role to preparing yourself and building your confidence for the moment you step in the interview room, you will see exactly how to keep your composure and impress.

Chapter 3, Some Difficult Questions You'll Face at the Interview, explores the different types of questions you might face in an interview and equips you with strategies to answer them that underline your strengths without taking you outside of your comfort zone as an introvert. You will see how to present your introversion with confidence and aplomb, demonstrating the skills and knowledge you can bring to the role.

Who this book is for

If you are looking for your dream job or to move your career forward but feel anxious and slightly daunted at the thought of networking and self-promotion, this book will demonstrate how you can successfully find and get the job you want—and deserve—by harnessing rather than hiding your introversion.

Conventions

In this book, you will find a number of styles of text that distinguish between different kinds of information. Here are some examples of these styles, and an explanation of their meaning.

New terms and **important words** are shown in bold.

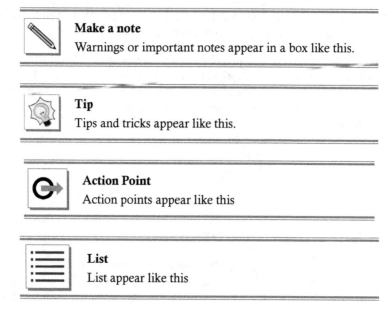

> **Make a note**
>
> Warnings or important notes appear in a box like this.

> **Tip**
>
> Tips and tricks appear like this.

> **Action Point**
>
> Action points appear like this

> **List**
>
> List appear like this

Reader feedback

Feedback from our readers is always welcome. Let us know what you think about this book—what you liked or may have disliked. Reader feedback is important for us to develop titles that you really get the most out of.

To send us general feedback, simply send an e-mail to feedback@impacktpub.com, and mention the book title via the subject of your message.

If there is a book that you need and would like to see us publish, please send us a note via the **Submit Idea** form on https://www.impacktpub.com/#!/bookidea.

Piracy

Piracy of copyright material on the Internet is an ongoing problem across all media. At Packt, we take the protection of our copyright and licenses very seriously. If you come across any illegal copies of our works, in any form, on the Internet, please provide us with the location address or website name immediately so that we can pursue a remedy.

Please contact us at copyright@impacktpub.com with a link to the suspected pirated material.

We appreciate your help in protecting our authors, and our ability to bring you valuable content.

Before the Interview

You've learned about what it means to be an introvert. Now you'll learn what paves the way to the interview and what strengths introverts use in the job search, as well as what challenges they face. Introverts will rely on their strengths in written communications, focus, and research. On the other hand, they'll have to get outside their comfort zone when it's time to network. Networking might be a challenge to introverts because it can require an outgoing demeanor and the ability to make small talk. As introversion speaks to the energy level of an individual, introverts may be required to forego their downtime, something they truly value, to attend networking events. Their verbal communication skills will be challenged. In this chapter, you'll learn how introverts can excel at writing CVs and other written documents, and how they can face the challenges presented in networking.

All of this is possible. In fact, during the most important time in your life—getting to the interview and winning the job—you can rise to the occasion. You need to remember that you are adaptable and that you can access your extrovert traits. Let's break down the job search and examine your strengths, while also being realistic about possible challenges.

Doing your research

Your first contact with the employer will most likely be your CV and possibly your cover letter. However, in order to write a CV that lands an interview, you'll need to research the jobs for which you're applying. Because of your abilities to be alone, prioritize, and focus on getting things accomplished, this should not be difficult to muster. Introverts are not averse to being alone, so use this alone time and put it to good use. Create an area in your home where you won't be disturbed, where you can keep your job-search materials nicely organized. Everything should be easily accessible. Your priorities should include learning as much about each job, which requires dissecting the job descriptions to better understand the most important skills required for each job. More good news about your research is it will also lend well to preparing for interviews. In the next chapter, we'll look at how to research the position and company in greater detail.

Make a note

Caveat: A challenge for introverts can be their tendency to spend more time on research than necessary. Don't dwell on every nuance and small detail. You must keep this point in mind, as dwelling on every small detail can result in failing to deliver the CV and other documents before the deadline.

Your personal marketing campaign

When you think about how businesses succeed, it's because they have great products or services and outstanding marketing. You must now think of yourself as a business that is selling a great product: you. Your marketing campaign will consist of written and verbal communication skills, both of which need to come together to conduct a successful marketing campaign that will get you to the interview. Beginning with your written communications, you have four possible documents: the CV, cover letter, approach letter, and LinkedIn profile. Your verbal communications will be tested with personal networking, informational interviews, follow ups, and finally the interview, which will be discussed in the next chapter. Let's break these down in this chapter.

Written communications

Introverts tend to excel at written communications because it allows them to take time to formulate their ideas. This is where you might be more comfortable, compared to the verbal communications side of your marketing communications. Of the four documents we'll look at, the CV is the most common example of written communications, and the component many people focus on the most. However, don't neglect the cover letter, approach letter, and LinkedIn profile.

The CV

As mentioned in the preface, introverts are frequently found to have a strong preference for writing and, therefore, do it extremely well. But in order to write a powerful CV, you must research the position by reading the job description and determining the major requirements. A detailed job description should not intimidate you; rather, it should give you the information you need to construct a powerful CV. Your research will also be necessary to write cover letters and approach letters. Introverts are great researchers because they are patient, persistent, and focused on their goal of creating a powerful CV. (Because the CV is your most important job-search document, I'll spend more time addressing it than the other documents.)

The most important elements of the CV

> *No one ever reads a [CV] unless they have to; they have to because a specific job has been titled and carefully defined, a salary range has been agreed upon, the position has been budgeted and approved, and the funds released.*

> –Martin Yate, *Knock 'em Dead Resumes*

Contrary to what many believe, no one likes reading a pile of CVs. Imagine having to read 75 CVs—no, simply imagine reading 25 CVs—to determine which eight people you'll invite for an interview. Before long you'll want to push the CVs aside and get back to what really excites you about work. This is how most hiring managers feel; they'd rather be doing something else and will find any reason to not read another CV. But reading CVs is an important aspect of their job because the only way they'll know who to invite for an interview is by reading these CVs, yours included. The most pressing need they have at the moment is filling a position with someone like you.

When I ask senior- and mid-level jobseekers in my workshop if they enjoyed reading CVs as part of their job, at least 98 percent said they didn't. They confirmed that the majority of the CVs were poorly formatted, badly written, failed to hit the mark in terms of their needs, and probably worst of all, people sometimes lied about their past. This paints a bleak picture of reading CVs, but this is my intention; you have to make your CV more enjoyable to read by doing the following:

> ➤ Making your CV easy to read
> ➤ Tailoring your CV to a particular job
> ➤ Prioritizing statements
> ➤ Highlighting your accomplishments
> ➤ Making it the proper length

Making your CV easy to read

As we just mentioned, employers receive more CVs than they'd prefer to read, so readability is one of their main requirements in a CV. This means that paragraphs should not exceed three or four lines; they should not resemble lengthy paragraphs in a Charles Dickens novel. Important points you need to make should be easy to grasp at a very quick glance because something you may not have been told is that the first read of a CV is a 6 to 10 second scan of your document.

Use strong action verbs at the beginning of each paragraph to grab the employer's attention. Words such as "developed," "initiated," "directed," "created," "engineered," and "motivated" are a few powerful verbs you can use. Sprinkling **bold text** in your CV's sentences is another way to make it easier for employers to identify important strategic words and phrases, namely accomplishments you want to highlight.

Bullet points also make it easier for the reviewer of your CV to capture essential information. However, try not to write a CV that consists entirely of bullet points. Doing this will make it appear more like a grocery list which may blur duty statements with accomplishments. A contrast between bullets and paragraphs gives your CV a more appealing look.

Tailoring your CV to a particular job

This is something many people fail to do because they don't take the time to research the job's requirements. As an introvert, you will employ your ability to focus and research skills to create a unique CV, not a one-size-fits-all document that doesn't consider the needs and problems the employer is facing. Make sure you make note of the major requirements and address them, demonstrating your qualifications for that specific position. Writing a tailored CV takes more work because you'll rewrite the performance profile and in some cases the work history, but it's worth the extra effort. Remember that employers are not terribly excited about reading a slew of CVs. This will cause them to take note of the extra work you've put into constructing your CV. It will make reading your CV more enjoyable. As mentioned before, it will nicely set you up for the interview.

Prioritize statements

Readability and constructing a unique CV are important, but they aren't the only important considerations. In addition, you must show that you understand the needs of the employer by covering the position's requirements in order of importance. For example, if you ascertain, by carefully dissecting the job description, that verbal and written communications are the top skills, you will list them as your top qualifications in your performance profile. Customer service is second in importance, so you list this skill as your second qualification. Creating web content is third, so you'll show your proficiency in developing web content. You get the point. Further, you will continue prioritizing statements throughout your CV, including your work history. Don't be concerned that you'll have to totally construct a new work history; it may only require rearranging a few bullet points here and there. Introverts pay attention to details and are meticulous in their approach to writing, so this third rule of writing a CV will not be difficult to master.

Highlighting your accomplishments

Perhaps the most important feature of a strong CV is the abundance of relevant quantified accomplishments. These speak volumes to employers who are trying to separate the ordinary from the extraordinary. Employers are no longer impressed with duty statements; they want to see how job candidates have increased revenue, saved costs and time, improved productivity, solved problems, and other types of accomplishments. It's best when stating your accomplishments that you quantify them by using numbers, dollars, and percentages. This proves your assertions in a clear and factual way. For instance, you may write, "Saved costs by training staff on accounting software." This sounds fine, but there are still questions to be answered. Alternatively, and more effectively, you could state your accomplishment like this: "Saved $12,500 in outside training costs by voluntarily training staff on new accounting software." The first example of an accomplishment fails to impress, while the second one demonstrates quantified value and paints a complete picture.

Not only must you be able to write about your quantified accomplishments; you must also talk about them while networking and at the interview. Introverts have the time to think about them and explain them through their CV but must also commit them to memory when it's time to speak about them.

Proper length

In addition to readability, tailoring your CVs, prioritizing statements, and highlighting accomplishments, you must consider the length of your CV. This again makes the job of reading many CVs easier on the employer. Generally speaking, two pages should be the maximum length for a CV. A one-page CV may be preferred, but you don't want to leave out important information by writing a one-pager. As long as you can capture the employer's attention in the first third of your CV, the employer will read your two-page CV. People with less than five years of work experience may be better off writing a one-page CV, rather than attempting to fill it with fluff or irrelevant information.

Make a note

Some of my executive-level jobseekers submit a one-page, accomplishment-based CV to the employer, and make their four-page CV available if called for.

The cover letter

We've looked at the most important document you'll write for the job search. Now let's address the cover letter. Writing this document will require as much research and dedicated alone time as the CV takes. Because of their preference for writing, introverts generally don't see this as as much of a burden as extroverts might. Researching the position and company is a necessity because the cover letter must be tailored to each job for which you apply.

You may have heard that the cover letter is not read by employers. This is partly true, as recruiters, hiring managers, and HR are bogged down by a stack of CVs; but experts attest that at least 50 percent of hiring authorities still read cover letters. Why do they read cover letters? Hiring authorities read cover letters because they provide a more expansive picture of the job candidate. Cover letters tell a story that can't be completely told by the CV. Another thing you should consider before choosing not to send a cover letter is that if you don't send one, you'll be one of the few who do not. This will not bode well on your dedication and interest in the job.

Have you ever been asked, "Why do you want to work at this company?" or some derivative of this question? I'm sure you have. The cover letter is a perfect place to explain this. Also, the cover letter explains why you want to take on the responsibility of the position. In other words, the cover letter shows your enthusiasm for the position and working for the company.

Another purpose of the cover letter is to highlight relevant accomplishments found on your CV. The word "relevant" is noteworthy because relevant accomplishments tell employers not only what you've done in the past, but they also tell them what you will do for them in the future. This is particularly true if you have multiple relevant accomplishments. Take an employer, for example, whose main concern is increasing accuracy in the accounting department. Your four examples of how you've accomplished this will be proof of what you've done in the past, and shows what you're capable of doing in the future.

The approach letter

The two most important documents you'll send to an employer in response to an advertised position are the CV and cover letter. But what about the jobs that aren't advertised, the ones that exist in the **Hidden Job Market** (**HJM**)? It's estimated that nearly 75 percent to 80 percent of all jobs are unadvertised. Smart jobseekers find those jobs through networking.

This is where the approach letter comes in. This document is not often used, which is a shame, as it's a great networking tool for introverts. Here's why the approach letter is not often used: the majority of jobseekers are pursuing the 25 percent of jobs that are advertised. In other words, only the smart jobseekers are using approach letters.

Approach letters are sent to companies that haven't advertised a position. It is a knock on the door, but a knock on the door that introverts feel more comfortable with. The approach letter is only sent to companies for which you'd like to work. You are taking your job search into your own hands because you're not reacting to advertised positions—which, again, most jobseekers are pursuing. You're being more proactive, and this is a good thing.

The approach letter appeals to introverts because it's a way for them to network by using their written communication skills, precluding the need for them to pick up the phone and make a call to the companies. Extroverts are more inclined to pick up the phone or even visit the company; however, remember that companies these days have gatekeepers (a receptionist, say) who are instructed to turn all jobseekers away. Who do you send your approach letter to, you may wonder. Generally, you'll send it to someone who will take notice, such as a hiring manager or someone higher up, say the president of the company. By no means should you send an approach letter to HR. They will simply place your letter in the circular file cabinet.

You may have guessed by now that the approach letter will require you to do research on the organization and position in which you're interested. You must give the recipient of your letter a reason to invite you in for a discussion. Show them your knowledge and appreciation for the company, as well as your related experience and accomplishments, of course.

The LinkedIn profile

Resembles the CV

It is widely believed that LinkedIn is the best, most professional online networking tool. LinkedIn has more than 300 million members and is growing at a rate of two new members a second. Therefore, you should join the LinkedIn craze and give yourself a chance to be found by employers who are looking for people with your talent. To call the LinkedIn profile a part of your written communications is accurate because you are, in fact, writing a profile which resembles the CV...to an extent. Let me elaborate on this point. At first you may want to copy and paste the content of your CV, and then modify it so it is a networking document.

An effective LinkedIn profile will contain many of the elements of a CV, such as a compelling *Summary*, a descriptive *Employment* section, and a complete *Education* section. But other features of the LinkedIn profile turn it into more of a networking tool than the CV. For example, in many countries a photo is not included on the CV, whereas members of LinkedIn are highly encouraged to include one. This gives LinkedIn more of a personal touch than the CV, and many people prefer it over the CV for this personal touch. There are other components of the profile that differ from the CV, such as the *Media* section (your online portfolio), *Skills and Expertise* and *Endorsements*, the *Recommendations* section, and *Interests*.

Requires constant activity

To be successful, introverts must be active on LinkedIn and venture beyond creating their online CV. They must post updates, send direct messages, participate in groups, respond to updates, and so on. Too often LinkedIn members create their profile and then wait for visitors to come to them. When my workshop attendees ask me how many updates are enough, I tell them at least one a day is the minimum amount. This seems like a lot to them, but I go through an exercise during the workshop where I'll post three updates within five minutes. The LinkedIn profile is static, unlike your CV which should be tailored to each job, so communicating with your network is essential to staying in their minds.

Appeal to introverts

Introverts may find solace in LinkedIn because of the hours a day they can spend on writing their profile and posting updates. This activity can be seen as the introverts' way of corresponding with their connections. More to the point, LinkedIn allows them to engage in online networking without having to reach out and speak to their connections, if they so desire. This is a mistake. While you may connect with hundreds or thousands of people on LinkedIn, they don't become *bona fide* connections unless you personally reach out to them by calling or even getting together with them for coffee or lunch. Extroverts are comfortable with reaching out and meeting with people, even connections they've met for the first time on LinkedIn.

Introverts should follow their counterparts' lead when it comes to personal networking, as personal networking is the best method to use to get to the interview. Allow me to repeat: you can develop your online network to include hundreds or thousands of connections, but they will not be bona fide connections unless you reach out to them in a personal manner.

Verbal communications

We've looked the written communications side of your job-search marketing campaign, which can consist of the CV, cover letter, approach letter, and LinkedIn profile. But these components are only half of the equation. The other half is your verbal communications which, as mentioned earlier, can be challenging for introverts if they're not properly prepared. This part of the chapter will examine the various ways to network, including events, day-to-day, and informational meetings.

Networking

You've learned that introverts feel more comfortable communicating through writing and do it quite well. Introverts are also capable of succeeding at personal networking; they simply go about it differently than their more outgoing counterparts, the extrovert. Generally put, introverts prefer smaller groups and deeper conversations, whereas extroverts prefer larger groups and broader conversation. Introverts are also said to be better listeners than extrovert, who are said to be better at making small talk. In case you're wondering, pundits estimate that networking can account for 60 percent of a jobseeker's success as the only method used to find a job. There are various ways to network.

Various types of networking

Networking events

When we think of networking, we picture networking events where jobseekers gather in a large room or hall to converse with each other. They deliver their stiff elevator pitch, talk about their accomplishments, and wander from person to person working the room. This is one way to view networking; however, it is an unfavorable way to envision networking. Even most extroverts will agree that this idea of networking is uncomfortable, if not downright intimidating. In fact, networking conducted this way is counterintuitive for introverts and extrovert alike. It is contrived and allows very little room to develop long-lasting relationships. Nonetheless, this type of networking is common in every city and most towns, and it will most likely continue to exist till the end of time. Should you refrain from this type of networking? Certainly not. Just keep in mind that you will need to have clear goals before you enter the networking event.

One goal is determining how many people with whom you will speak. The number may be three, two, or even just one. Remember that introverts prefer to speak with fewer people, yet engage in deeper conversations. Don't feel as if you have to emulate extroverts who enjoy meeting many people and having briefer conversations. This is not your style.

Another goal is trying to help some of the individuals at the event by offering a lead to a possible position, or informing the folks of other people with whom they may like to meet. Understanding the needs of your fellow networkers can only be accomplished through—one of the introverts' many strengths—active listening. Go to the event with the attitude that you're there to help first and receive help second.

The third goal is simply "**Do It**."

Remember to bring personal business cards, which are cards similar to the ones you had when working, but are more about you as a jobseeker or a business owner. Let's say you've worked in Marketing. Naturally, you'll have your contact information listed on your cards—perhaps including your LinkedIn URL. But people will need to know what your areas of strength are. Are you strong in public relations, web content, social media, and vendor relations? Clearly state this on your personal business card. To arrive without a business card will be quite embarrassing, so make up a personal business card right away.

Day-to-day networking

Think about what you do when you need a good babysitter, a trustworthy mechanic, advice on what movie to see, someone to shovel your walkway after a snow storm, and other needs you may have. You ask people whom you trust. Or, if like me, you asked a complete stranger where she had her Honda serviced—which incidentally turned out to be the best advice I ever received. This is how we network on a daily basis without giving it much thought. And this is how networking for work should be done. This method is so easy to do, yet many jobseekers fail to do it.

But there is etiquette introverts must follow when networking day-to-day. It involves two rules. First, tell everyone you know that you're looking for a new job, and be clear about your experience and needs. Second, resist the urge to make all your conversations about your job search, and resist the urge to ask people if they know of any jobs. The second rule may seem counterproductive, but you don't want to drive every friend, neighbor, and relative away by violating this rule.

"It's not what you know, it's who you know. " You've heard this phrase before. Remember that introverts feel most comfortable in small groups that allow for deeper conversation. From your networking events, you may meet people who would like to meet for coffee or tea one time a week, where you can discuss your job search, offer advice, ideas, and leads.

Don't be afraid to make phone calls or send an e-mail to your connections, who essentially are everyone you know. Call them to simply check-in, congratulate them on their birthday, ask how their son's football game went, and so on. But don't alienate them by always asking if they've heard about a job suitable for you. They know your employment situation because they'll ask you how you're doing. At this point it's proper to say something like, "I'm still looking for a job as an accountant manager." These simple "pings" will keep you in their mind. One of my former customers constantly sent me e-mails to update me on his job search. He always remained positive. So when I learned of opportunities, I alerted him to them, simply because he remained in my mind.

Here's how Nancy Ancowitz, *Self-Promotion for Introverts*, encourages introverts to look at networking:

> *"As an introvert, you'd probably rather listen than talk most of the time. You're adept at building deep and lasting relationships. You're trusted, accountable, and a core contributor. However, you're not a schmoozer. You value your space and quiet time. Regardless, you have distinct advantages that enable you to create a strong network that can provide you with continuous support. "*

Informational interviews

One of the most underused ways to network is the informational interview, or what I prefer to call, **informational meetings**. The distinction is small and the process is the same, but "informational interview" implies to the person who's giving you advice that it's an interview, when it's really a meeting that should be relaxed, yet informative. Nonetheless, this is a meeting you ask someone at a company you're interested in working for if you can sit with them to gather information on a position and the company. You bring the questions, so make them intelligent questions. This meeting should create a relaxed environment—after all, you're not being interviewed, and the person granting you the informational meeting is under no pressure to hire you. The ultimate outcome of a meeting like this would be you being recommended to the hiring manager if a position is developing in the company, or being kept in mind for positions in the future. At the very least, you should leave with two or three other people with whom you could speak. This type of meeting is a great way to penetrate the Hidden Job Market.

Follow up

You've attended networking events, networked daily with everyone you know, and conducted some informational meetings. Now it's time to follow up with the people with whom you've spoken. Your correspondence with these connections can be delivered in the form of e-mails first, followed by a phone conversation where you'll set up a face-to-face meeting. Following up is incredibly important because it solidifies the connections you've made. Some believe that as many as seven correspondences are necessary to solidify a connection. No matter what the number, be sure to send that e-mail or make the call.
If there proves to be no substantial commonality between you and the person you met, there's no need to follow through with a personal meeting.

Summary

In this chapter, we looked at ways to get to the interview, including the documents that comprise your written communications: CV, cover letter, approach letter, and LinkedIn profile; as well as your verbal communications, for example, the various types of networking. All these components need to come together in order for you to be successful in your journey to the interview.

In the next chapter, we will look at the interview exclusively. You will be glad to know that you can put your research skills to use *before* attending the interview. So, we'll spend more time looking at how to effectively research the position and company, as well as the competition. However, at the interview—telephone or face-to-face—you will be called on to use your extrovert traits, such as making small talk, demonstrating enthusiasm, and exuding confidence. You can succeed at the interview and win the job if you put your mind to it.

>2

You've Landed the Interview, Now What?

The excitement is so great you can hardly contain yourself. You've landed an interview at a company for which you want to work and, most importantly, a position that's perfect for you. On the other hand, you might dread the interview, where you'll have to think quickly on your feet and engage in small talk, which is sometimes a challenge for introverts.

In the previous chapter, we looked at the importance of conducting an effective job search in order to get to the ultimate prize, the interview. It is the interview that wins you the job. It is the interview where you must be at your best, where your first impressions must endear you to the employer, where you must answer the difficult questions. What you did before the interview—conducting the research, submitting a powerful CV and cover letter, utilizing LinkedIn, and networking face-to-face—has paid off. There are a few more details you have to take care of before you're ready to take the hot seat and earn your next position.

In this chapter, you'll learn what steps to take leading up to the interview. If you guessed research is one of them, you are correct. Research was important when you were preparing to land the interview with a powerful CV; now it's an important step in acing the interview. Preparation in the form of assembling your outfit, locating the company, and more is also something you'll need to do if you want to walk into the room confident and calm.

More importantly, you'll learn about what to expect at the interview; the importance of first impressions, such as eye contact and the handshake; answering the tough questions. Are you familiar with behavioral-based questions? Concluding the interview with questions for the interviewers will follow. This chapter will end with sending the thank you note, which is the most overlooked step in the interview process; a very important step, may I add.

Research

Research is familiar territory for introverts, as I've mentioned before. Introverts are very strong at research because of their ability to focus and use their alone time effectively. If you've noticed introverts at work, you will recall how they sit quietly at their desk, reading the text on the screen, and typing away. What you see is their ability to concentrate with the work at hand. This is how they learn best. The extroverts, on the other hand, are usually conversing with colleagues and exchanging information because this is how they learn best. Take advantage of the time you have to conduct the research you need to be prepared for the interview. You may require space at home, such as an office, where you can concentrate without disruptions; or you may conduct your research at a slightly noisy, yet comfortable, coffee shop. How your research is done is up to you; just make it a priority in preparing for the interview.

Before we go any further, I want to talk about *being selfish*. That's right, being selfish in order to get your research accomplished. I tell my jobseekers that the job search is about them. It's not about doing errands for others who say, "You're out of work. You can do this errand for me." Long-overdue projects around the house are also out of the question, unless they're activities that will take your mind off the job search for a bit of time. What will you be researching, you may wonder. I'm glad you asked. The first topic you'll research is the position.

Make a note

Caveat: Don't get bogged down in your research to the point where you become anxious and arrive at the interview more stressed out than needed. The goal is to be prepared.

The position

This is the most obvious research you'll conduct because the majority of the questions will be centered on the position at hand. The interviewer(s) will be asking questions regarding your **job-related skills**—known also as hard skills—**adaptive skills**—or personality skills—and **transferable skills**. It is essential that you're aware of these skills and can address them at the interview, particularly the skills you've identified as important to the position. Let's say, for instance, you've identified the following skills as important: written and verbal communications, customer service, social media, organization, and so on. These are the skills you'll most likely need to address at the interview. You'll need to recall how well you've performed the required skills to be able to answer questions from the interviewer about these skills.

Where do I find the skills that are essential to the position, you may be wondering. The most obvious answer would be the job ad which you saw on the Internet or in a newspaper. Let's look at an example of a partial job ad for a salesperson and determine which skills are most important for the position (the most important skills are written in bold text):

Excellent **written and verbal communication skills**; **interacts with and works well with others in various fast-changing environments/situations**; demonstrates **strong networking and listening skills**; effective **problem-solving skills**; able to **motivate others through persuasion and leadership**; able to **prioritize, manage time, and orchestrate multiple tasks simultaneously**; able to **maintain self-confidence and high self-esteem in tasks such as cold calling and prospecting**; able to effectively **work independently or in a team environment**; able to **maintain company and customer confidentiality**; practices **corporate and personal integrity** on the highest level ... Salary and commissions commensurate with contribution.

This job ad shows important skills for the position; these are the skills that you can assume will be addressed at the interview. Now list the skills in descending order of importance. Your required skills list will look like this:

- ➤ Written and verbal communication skills
- ➤ Interacts with and works well with others in various fast-changing environments/situations
- ➤ Strong networking and listening skills
- ➤ Problem-solving skills
- ➤ Motivate others through persuasion and leadership
- ➤ Prioritize, manage time, and orchestrate multiple tasks simultaneously
- ➤ Maintain self-confidence and high self-esteem in tasks such as cold calling and prospecting
- ➤ Work independently or in a team environment
- ➤ Maintain company and customer confidentiality
- ➤ Corporate and personal integrity

Now write a synopsis of how you've demonstrated these skills as preparation for the interview, because you're more likely to remember what you write. Write about times when you demonstrated written and verbal communication skills, interacted well with others... and so on. As an introvert, this is a welcome activity because you'll be using one of your preferred strengths, writing.

The company

The other topic of the interview will be the company/organization. It's important to know as much as you can about the company because you may be questioned about its products or services, mission statement, reputation, competition, and direction, among other aspects of the company. A simple solution to this would be visiting the company's website, but think about the nature of what's displayed on its website.

That's right, marketing literature. So, to get deeper in your research, you may want to see what's been printed about the company by using Google or other search engines, or talking with someone who works there. It's best to be prepared to answer some negative questions regarding the company; you'll never know when the interviewer may spring on you a question like, "Why do you think our stocks have gone down?"

Another reason why your extensive research on the company/organization is important is because it will demonstrate enthusiasm and motivation to work at said company. You will show you know more about the company than the other more outgoing applicants, perhaps making up for lack of enthusiasm in other ways, which we'll discuss a little later on. The bottom line is that employers want to be assured that you *want* to work for the company, not that you're just looking for any old job. During the interview, it would be wise beginning a statement with: "While I was researching your company, I discovered...." This will impress the interviewer(s) because you will come across as someone who is prepared, as well as interested in the company. It never hurts to boost the employer's ego, does it?

One other source to use when researching the company is LinkedIn, as many employees, including hiring managers, have LinkedIn profiles. You may want to visit their profiles to learn more about the people who will be interviewing you. You can learn important information about them, such as where they went to university, their interests, volunteer experience, and more. This information can be great fodder for conversation during the interview.

Preparation – approaching the interview

If you are called for an interview for the following day, do you have your interview outfit ready to go? Well, do you? Is your suit dry-cleaned; do you have a nicely pressed shirt or blouse; do you know where your shoes are, and are they polished; what will you wear for jewelry? You get the idea, right? You'll be surprised by how many people are caught off guard because they don't have their interview outfit prepared on a moment's notice. I think we've all had to run to the store to get a fresh shirt or blouse the night before an interview. This is enough to throw anyone off their game. When one of my friends passed away young, I searched in vain for my best suit to wear to his funeral, only to find it hanging in the back of another closet, rumpled and with a spot on it. Although it wasn't for an interview that I needed a freshly pressed suit, it was an important moment, nonetheless. Now I make sure that my suit is ready to go.

Clothes aside, there's the matter of practicing your interview answers and techniques. Introverts are master preparers because they understand how important it is to be in the proper frame of mind before an interview. They understand that when it comes to an interview, they need to prepare for the tough interview questions.

Remember the list of skills we came up with from the job ad for a salesperson. The first skills are verbal and written communications. The next essential skill is working well with others, and so on. Your task is to devise questions for each of the skills mentioned in the ad and to write the answers down. It's important to write the answers down because you'll remember your answers better. For the first skill, you may want to answer the question: "Tell me about a time when your written communication skills played a major role in securing an account." Or, "You are managing three accounts of great importance and one of the accounts wants to drop us due to a mistake your colleague made in pricing. What will you do?"

After you've written your answers for all the requisite skills, you should practice saying them in any manner you like: in front of a mirror, a friend, or relative; while you're out walking or driving; in the shower, and so on. Just be aware of people who may be watching you. You may get a few odd looks.

The best preparation for an interview, in my mind, is a **mock interview**. Your local career center or a job coach can help you tremendously by engaging you in a mock interview. The format is straightforward; the "mock" interviewer will ask you a series of questions without interruption and then at the end of the session will provide you feedback on your answers, body language, tone of voice, and other important aspects of your performance. To make this really work, you should supply the interviewer with a job description and your CV, so they can ask questions similar to what you'd be asked at the real interview. I have conducted many mock interviews with my jobseekers, and they have commented that mock interviews are the most effective way to prepare them for the real thing. They also said they were scared to death before the mock interview began but soon became comfortable. Just recently I conducted a mock interview with someone by using Skype. The biggest challenge for me was learning about Skype. But the mock interview went well, and I was able to give her advice on the content of her answers; her composure; and, unfortunately, her propensity to talk too much.

No one can say for sure when you'll be completely ready for the interview. The one thing you should count on, as an introvert, is that you've done your research and are prepared for the all-important interview. This might not be said about the extroverts, who tend to put less emphasis into their research and preparation and rely more on their confidence and outgoingness at the interview. With preparation, you should have the confidence that will guide you through the interview.

The last thing we need to address is your frame of mind. Plain and simple, the more relaxed and confident—because of your research—you are, the better you'll do at the interview. I suggest that all the research you conduct before the interview be done days in advance, so you'll have the opportunity to sleep well before the big day. You should also relax by having a nice dinner, perhaps with your spouse or friend, the night before. In other words, try to put the big day out of your mind. Cramming the night before the interview is like cramming before an exam, when you stayed up all night trying to pack all that information into your head. It never worked well for me as a student at university. Did it work well for you? Finally, if you need a pep talk, don't be afraid to ask for one from the person who will do the best job of it. I've been known to deliver great pep talks to my jobseekers who were nervous before the interview. I'll ask them, "Are you ready?" When they say they are, I'll say, "You'll get the offer."

First impressions

The old saying, "First impressions are everything" rings true in many cases. Sadly, many interviewers will decide to *not* hire a candidate within the first 30 seconds to 3 minutes, based on a poor first impression; so don't hurt your chances by arriving at an interview and making a poor first impression. In my mind, these interviewers who focus too much on first impressions are terrible at their job, but this is the reality of the hiring process.

Eye contact

Making steady eye contact is essential at interviews, as it tells the interviewer(s) that you are trustworthy, engaged, interested, enthusiastic, and aren't hiding something (to this last point, I think about when young children are hiding the fact that they broke a window with their football). Your eye contact is part of your communications; in other words, you can speak with your eyes. Eyes wide open can indicate excitement and happiness, while slightly closed eyes can indicate disapproval and even anger. Do you see the importance of eye contact now?

There's no evidence that introverts are less capable of making eye contact than extroverts, but the nature of introverts' reflectiveness may indicate deeper and lingering eye contact. As an introvert, be aware of the length of your eye contact. Don't intimidate the interviewer(s) by intensely staring at them. At the same time, don't divert your eyes too often. My jobseekers often ask me if it's acceptable to look away occasionally; to which I tell them that it is, especially if they're contemplating an answer. Interviewers understand you'll need time to think a bit longer about some of the difficult questions they pose. Who you maintain eye contact with when there are multiple interviewers is important, as well. When you're asked a question, the majority of your eye contact should be directed toward the interviewer who asked the question, but don't neglect the others in the room; that is simply impolite.

The handshake

Eye contact ranks very high as far as first impressions go, but the handshake is just as important. The general rule on handshakes is to deliver one that is firm yet gentle. If you're wondering what I mean by this, let me tell you of a time when I shook an elderly woman's hand and I swore I heard the bones in her hand crack. My suspicion was confirmed when I saw her wince in pain. Please keep in mind that some people may have arthritis or just simply have brittle bones. So a handshake that nicely envelops the hand is preferred. Other handshakes people don't appreciate are limp; wet palm; lingering; and my pet peeve, the who-can-grab-the-other-person's-hand-first handshake. I don't like being grabbed by my fingers unable to grasp the other person's hand. I feel so strongly about the handshake that I judge a person's character by it.

However, many countries have different traditions—BBC Capital asserts that handshakes in the United Kingdom are not as firm as those in the U.S.; in the UAE, the handshake lingers for as long as the initiator desires; and in China, the handshake is accompanied by a slight bow. If these factoids tell us anything, it's that handshakes do have significance to various cultures.

Who shakes whose hand first? There is some debate when it comes to the opposite gender as to who should extend his or her hand first. Depending on the culture, it may not matter if the woman shakes the man's hand first. In the U.S., it is perfectly fine for the woman to extend her hand first and deliver a firm yet gentle handshake. It is a sign of assertiveness, an important trait in the business world.

Smile

Introverts are by nature reflective and thoughtful, so smiling at a tense moment, such as an interview, may not come as natural to them. Extroverts, on the other hand, enjoy the opportunity to strut their stuff, so they're more apt to smile and maintain their smile. It's important for introverts to remember to smile; in other words, act more extroverted. A friendly smile shows enthusiasm. It tells interviewers that you're happy to be there. Most people are naturally drawn more to people who smile than those who don't. But don't force a smile that comes across as fake; you'll just make matters worse. Try thinking of happy moments in your life that take you away from the stressful situation in which you're in. Don't continuously smile like a Cheshire cat either, as this will come across as disingenuous, especially at moments when reflection and thoughtfulness are required, such as when you're asked, "What is your greatest weakness?"

Do you know people who never smile? I'm sure you do. Does this mean they're unhappy people? Certainly not. Some people by nature don't smile, yet they're happy. If you're the type who doesn't smile, show your enthusiasm for the position by bringing more information to the table. Other candidates may smile like fools; but if you show more knowledge of the position and the company, you'll appear as someone who is more than capable of performing the duties, as well as someone who will be a pleasure with whom to work.

Where to sit and your posture

You've entered the room where you'll be interviewed before the people who are conducting the interview. There are six chairs positioned around the large mahogany table, and you're wondering where you should sit. Let's put your worries to rest by suggesting that you wait to be seated. Your interviewers will tell you where you should sit, or you can simply ask them; but by no means should you take any seat you'd like. This is one time when assertiveness is not required. Can you imagine sitting in the lead interviewer's chair? She would not appreciate that.

Do you accept the cup of water they offer you? The obvious answer is yes, regardless of whether you'll drink it or leave it on the table in front of you. Most job candidates develop a dry throat, so it's wise to accept the offer— it's also the polite thing to do.

How you sit is also important. Interviewers will observe your posture and body language, so be cognizant of how straight you're sitting and if you are fidgeting with your fingers or hands or even tapping your feet. There are two acceptable ways to sit. The first is an upright position that is relaxed and not stiff. The second is leaning forward slightly, which shows interest and engagement. When leaning forward be sure you're not encroaching upon the interviewers' space. By no means should you slouch in your chair or lean back.

Candidates who are fidgety can be distracting almost to the point of annoying to the interviewer(s). So if you are someone who fidgets due to nervousness, find a comfortable position for your hands, perhaps in front of you on the table or even on your lap. Either is fine, though placing them on the table is preferred, as it allows you the ability to gesture with your hands (which can be an effective way to communicate if not overdone). One method I suggest to my jobseekers if they're concerned about fidgeting is to hold a pen that they've brought to the interview with which to take notes. I suggest that the pen you bring to the interview is not a click pen, or that you don't use to tap on the table. These can be a major distraction to the interviewer, and you may not know you're even doing it.

Small talk

Small talk is an area where introverts are not as comfortable as their bold and outgoing counterparts, the extroverts, and a lack of comfort in this area can pose a problem. Small talk can be a very important part of the interview. In some cases, it can be a deal breaker or deal maker. Your ability to engage in small talk speaks to your verbal communication skills, ability to reason, and how well you think quickly on your feet. If this is important to the interviewer(s), they'll be paying close attention to how well you can interact quickly and naturally. What is your knowledge of current events, sports, global business, what's important to their company? You may be asked to talk about all of this before the interview even begins. Or maybe you'll have interviewers who want to get right to the interview and will begin it with the directive, "Tell me about yourself." For the introvert—for you—it might be better this way.

But let's prepare for the small talk you might be asked to engage in. Here again your strong ability to research can play a significant role in how you manage your small talk. Let's say the company announced the day before your interview that it will contribute a fair sum of money to a charity. Perfect. This is your opportunity to start the small talk, while also showing your knowledge of the company. Make certain that you know the whole story, as the interviewer may decide to carry the conversation further than your declaration of the company's philanthropic endeavors. In addition to reading the daily news, you'll also want to follow what's going on at the company. Starting the small talk with information you've read on the company can be a great way to get to the chase of what you know about the company.

You need to be a super sleuth when you enter the interview room. Look about the room and take note of what's hanging on the walls, sitting on the desk or table. Are there photos of family members, interesting paintings, a photo of Wembley Stadium, a clay statue of a Tutu warrior? Be your introverted self and instead of blurting out whatever comes to mind as you walk in the room, take time to observe the room, formulate your thoughts, and then make an intelligent statement. "I see you have a painting of Monet's 'Water

Lilies.' One of my favorites." Follow with an open-ended question demonstrating your interest in other people and ability to listen actively.

Your small talk doesn't need to be only about the company. You may be a sports fan and sense the interviewer(s) are as well. Mentioning how well Arsenal is doing compared to Manchester United can be perfectly fine, as long as the interviewer(s) are not avid Manchester United fans. In the U.S., saying disparaging things about the Yankees when in the presence of a Yankees fan might not be wise either.

Avoid negative comments. If your ride to the interview was fraught with traffic or you got a bit lost, don't mention these facts. Instead, tell the interviewer(s) that your journey was just fine. You don't want to come across as someone who complains or lets little matters upset you. Other topics to avoid are religion and politics, as you'll never know on which end of the spectrum your interviewer(s) fall; or if they're even interested in talking about such topics.

Types of interviews

Let's talk about various types of interviews before getting into the categories of tough questions. Today's interviewers use a variety of interview styles to hire the most qualified candidates. We'll look at four of the most common types of interviews:

➤ One-on-one
➤ Group
➤ Situational
➤ Telephone

One-on-one

These are interviews where you meet with one person. You will most likely sit across from this person, but don't be surprised if the interviewer would like you to sit side-by-side with them. I recall being interviewed in this manner and feeling uncomfortable as the interviewer, my future boss, sat closer than most interviewers would. Nonetheless, these types of interviews give you the opportunity to size up the interviewer, determining whether they are open and friendly, most likely an extrovert, or serious and to-the-point, most likely an introvert. Knowing whether the interviewer is an introvert or extrovert may help you determine how long or short your answers should be. Most extroverts are open to longer answers and may follow up their questions with additional ones, whereas introverts usually prefer shorter answers from the candidate. Regardless, the proper length of your answers should not exceed two minutes.

One-on-one interviews tend to be those conducted by the hiring manager or the person with the final word. One word of advice is that you may be asked questions that are inappropriate or even illegal. Examples of these might be questions about your age, race, gender, marital status, possible disability, and nationality. If you receive questions like these, you can choose to refuse to answer them or answer them honestly, then following up your answer with a reason why your age, for example, is a benefit to the employer.

Choosing not to answer the question may be seen as confrontational. One might answer the age question with, "Well, I'm 50 years old. And I've been told that my production rate is higher than that of someone half my age. Additionally, I bring to this company more years of job-related experience, life experience, and a sense of responsibility and dependability."

It's been my experience that the hiring managers are the interviewers who tend to ask inappropriate, if not illegal, questions for two major reasons. The first is their lack of training in interviewing job candidates. They may not know that it's inappropriate to ask a candidate what their religion is, or how many children the person has, or if the candidate is on medication for a visible disability. The other reason is their disdain for interviewing. Most hiring managers will tell you they'd rather be doing something else than asking eight people the same questions during sessions that take up a good part of their week. They are wasting time, they feel, without realizing they have one major problem to solve—to hire the person that will make their job easier.

Group interviews

Imagine walking into a room expecting to see one person sitting behind their desk, ready to extend their hand and welcome you to the company; but, instead, you are welcomed by six people who will be interviewing you. You'll be taken off guard and the game will be over, unless you're prepared for the group interview. Many of my jobseekers fear group interviews for no logical reason. I've conducted group interviews and been to them; and the only difference I see is that you're being interviewed by more than one person. The secret is focus.

Why do companies conduct group interviews? Group interviews are a benefit to the employer because they save time and costs. A group interview may consist of two, three, four, or five interviewers or more. They all hear the same answer to their questions and, therefore, can accurately rate the job candidates' abilities. Plus they don't have to schedule time to meet with each other to discuss their findings—they can do that immediately after each interview. Companies save money because, as the saying goes, "Time is money."

As the candidate, your job is to maintain proper etiquette by addressing each interviewer as individuals, which means you will make eye contact with everyone when you're answering a question, not only the person who asked it. In cases when each interviewer has a certain number of questions he or she has to ask (say five each), your answers will be concise, yet compelling. There will be little room for follow-up questions; and the interview may seem more like an interrogation. No worries. Each candidate is going through the same process because the interviewers want consistency in the types of questions, thereby creating a fair playing field. These types of panel interviews are common in academia, non-profits, medical, law enforcement, the military, and other sectors where objectivity is required.

On rare occasions you may find yourself being interviewed with a number of your peers, again a way for companies/organizations to save money and time; but also a way for them to see how you'll interact with other candidates. As an introvert you must demonstrate extroverted assertiveness by showing as much enthusiasm as your peers, not taking too much time to answer the questions from the interviewers, and engaging in rebuttal when appropriate. I'm not implying you must dominate the conversation—practice etiquette but don't back down. Also keep in mind that your peers will be as nervous, or more nervous, as you.

Situational interviews

Situational interviews are conducted when companies want to determine if the candidates can perform tasks that will be required of the position. There are specific situational questions, but we'll cover these in the *Types of questions you may face* section. If you ask an engineer, teacher, or a truck driver if they had to perform a job-related task at the interview, they'd certainly say they did. This makes perfect sense for an employer to test an engineer's ability to solve equations by having them perform the task in front of their interviewer(s). A teacher would have to develop a lesson plan for a one-hour period or a whole school day and teach it to the principal, faculty, and the students. My customers have been subjected to creating a presentation and then delivering it to the hiring manager, president of the company, and CFO for a project manager role.

For introverts, these interviews can be welcome, particularly if you are informed before the interview that you will be performing certain tasks. This will give you time to prepare for said assignments. Don't be alarmed if you have to present a marketing campaign to the VP of marketing at a bank or other business. Your ability to speak in public is as strong as an extrovert's. Multiple consecutive presentations are more of a concern, as it speaks to your energy level, not your ability to speak articulately.

Make a note

Many people with whom I speak falsely assume that introverts don't possess the ability to speak as eloquently as extroverts. Many great speakers are introverts, and those introverts will tell you that they need time to recharge their batteries after a series of workshops or lectures.

Telephone interviews

Telephone interviews, once used by employers only to determine your salary requirements and ability to perform technical tasks, are now similar to face-to-face interviews in the nature of the questions and frequency. Certainly a company wants to know what you expect for salary, but now more challenging questions are asked during telephone interviews, including behavioral-based questions which will be discussed later in this chapter. As an introvert, again you have the advantage of preparation. You will prepare for the telephone interview as you would the face-to-face interview. The difference is you won't meet the interviewer(s) at the company.

A customer of mine kept me apprised of his telephone interviews during the hiring process. After the fifth one he told me the good news; he'd been hired for a position and company he looked forward to working with. The twist was he was hired without having to meet anyone at the company. This is the point I'm making about the number and importance of the telephone interview.

Preparing for the telephone interview will play a key role in whether you're asked to meet the interviewers at the company, which is the goal of an interview process that can take weeks, if not months to complete. Some basic details to keep in mind include:

> ➤ Situate yourself in a comfortable area, free of noise and other distractions

> ➤ Have a copy of your CV and other documents by your side

> ➤ Make sure you won't lose the connection (a LAN line would probably be best)

> ➤ Answer the phone using your best phone manner

> ➤ Speak clearly and enunciate each word

> ➤ Listen very carefully to the questions being asked

> ➤ Ask the interviewer to repeat a question or two if you didn't hear or understand them

> ➤ Be concise while also providing compelling answers

> ➤ Be prepared to answer the tough questions

> ➤ At the end of the telephone interview, ask to meet with someone at the company for a face-to-face interview

Don't be surprised if you are asked to participate in a conference call, where a number of people will interview you, some in different parts of the world. Again, this is a way for people in different parts of the organization to ask you questions and hear the same answers. It's also a great way for the company to save costs.

Another common interview is one conducted using Skype or video conferencing. Companies conduct these interviews to get a look at how you appear and behave during the interview. You will have to have a web cam and sign up for Skype, a free program and used worldwide. Be certain that you have proper lighting and a plain background—certainly one that *doesn't* display photos of your children—and that you're dressed appropriately for the interview. Before they begin asking the questions, ask the interviewers where you should direct your eye contact, as the angle of the camera may not be in the direction that you think. Remember to smile.

The tough interview questions

Now that we've looked at the different types of interviews you'll face it's time to examine what makes or breaks your chances of getting the job. These, of course, are the questions you'll face.

The toughest questions you'll come across are the ones for which you're not prepared. Having done your research on the position, company, and competition, you should be well prepared to answer most, if not all, questions thrown your way. It's when introverts haven't done their research that they fail to answer the questions thrown at them. More than extroverts, introverts must do their research to be prepared and feel confident. Extroverts naturally feel confident and may forgo researching the position and company as thoroughly; but with their air of confidence, they might be able to pull off a fairly decent performance. The bottom line is that being prepared will give you the confidence you'll need to do well at the interview. Will you be nervous? Perhaps yes, perhaps no. Everyone experiences different emotions, but interviews, by their very nature, tend to make people nervous.

Ideally, the interview should not be an interview; rather, it should be a business meeting between the seller, whom is you, and the buyer, whom is the employer. Today's good interviewers realize that to get the best out of their candidates, they need to refrain from intimidating or even bullying them. Unfortunately, not all interviewers follow this model. They are usually the interviewers who choose the candidates who perform well under pressure but aren't necessarily the right candidates.

On the other hand, the best interviewers will come up with questions that get to the core of the job applicants. A great interviewer will combine three types of questions in general: **traditional**, **situational**, and **behavioral-based**. Let's examine why each type of question is asked, how to approach these questions, and some examples of the questions.

Traditional questions

Traditional questions are the most common type of questions. *"Why should we hire you?"* is one of the most common traditional questions, and I'm sure you've been asked this question at numerous interviews. The interviewer(s) ask this question because they want you to articulate the very reason why they're interviewing you, as well as to see if you can make a sound argument for being selected for the position. Some interviewers believe this is the best traditional question to ask, so be prepared to answer it. Another common traditional question is, *"What is your greatest weakness?"* This question is asked to see if you are aware of your strongest weakness, what you have done to correct this weakness, and if it is something you'll repeat. Interviewers also want to see how you'll react to this question. Will you answer it with clarity and assuredness, or will you crumble under the pressure? These are just two traditional questions you should expect to be asked, so do what an introvert would do: prepare for them. Let's look at some other common traditional questions.

"What are your career goals?" or "Where do you expect to be in five years?" are similar questions that are asked to determine if:

➤ You plan to stay with the company

➤ Whether you have goals

One might naturally assume that the interviewer wants to hear that you aspire to advance in the company, revealing ambitions; but you can show your ambition by demonstrating you'll help the company be its best by being an individual contributor or even taking a step back from your previous role as a manager. As long as you indicate that you'll take on major responsibilities and demonstrate innovation that will increase revenue, decrease cost, improve productivity, or accomplish a number of other goals, your answer will be regaled as a solid one. Remember, transparency and self-awareness are what employers want to hear from you.

"Tell me about yourself" is another question, or should we say directive, that many candidates face. They often struggle with this one because they don't have an elevator pitch prepared, in which they must stress their value to the employer through job-related responsibilities and accomplishments. Your answer doesn't have to exceed 30 seconds, but it must be a powerful statement of what greatness you'll bring to the company. One way to approach this directive is by saying something similar to this response:

"Based on my experience and many accomplishments, I will deliver the kind of performance you'd expect from a top salesman (think of the job description we examined at the beginning of this chapter). For the past five years, I have increased sales by 50 percent every year through my ability to communicate effectively with my major clients. In addition, I have been the person who my colleagues could come to with difficult questions and problems. My expertise in (whatever is required for the position) has saved the companies for which I worked time and needless costs. I can safely say that I will break into territories that will produce growth for this company, as I have in the past. Now that you know a little bit about me, I'd like to know what challenges your company is facing." Closing with a direct question can open up other discussions that will reveal what type of employee they are seeking, discussions that can help you structure your answers.

Traditional questions will also test your job-related, or technical, skills. Someone who is applying for a position that requires social media knowledge might be asked, "How have you used LinkedIn to develop relationships with potential partners?" As an introvert with experience in this arena, this is your opportunity to talk about how you have selectively sought potential connections in the sales and marketing segment. You will also tell the interviewer(s) how you have joined numerous groups in the medical industry, where you have contributed to discussions, becoming known as the thought leader in your field. Through your involvement on LinkedIn, you have developed more than 20 relationships with substantial partners, including five of the company's top partnerships. Oh, this was in addition to performing your other responsibilities at the highest level.

Many of my customers in the engineering fields recount two-hour sessions with hiring managers where they were drilled on how they would solve various equations. To the hiring managers, it's important that the candidates can hit the ground running, which means the candidates have the required technical skills.

Situational questions

We looked at the situational interview, in which you would have to perform a particular task; but I'd like to discuss a type of question you may face called a situational question. I won't spend a great deal of time going over the situational question, as it is similar to the traditional question in that candidates can deliver a canned answer—one they've prepared based on their knowledge of the position. Imagine if you're applying for a manager's position and the interviewer(s) says, "You approach two colleagues who are arguing in the office. What would you do in this situation?" The interviewer(s) objective is to determine if you can explain how you'd handle the situation, which doesn't necessarily mean you have done it. But that's beside the point. Your answer should be compelling enough to convince the interviewer(s) that you can perform certain tasks.

The best way to be prepared for situational questions is—you guessed it—to understand the requirements of the job. Other areas you could be tested on are how you set priorities, your interpersonal skills, how you would motivate others, teamwork, dealing with lack of resources, and so on.

The next type of question we'll look at is the behavioral-based question, which can strike fear in the heart of even the most experienced interviewee. This type of question requires exceptional recall as well as the ability to tell stories about how you have demonstrated the required skills.

Behavioral-based questions

Behavioral-based interview questions are not new to the interviewing scene. In fact, companies have conducted behavioral-based, sometimes called competency-based, interviews since the 1970s. They have proven to be more successful in finding the most qualified candidates because they get to the core of the candidate. As the name implies, this type of question's intent is to determine the nature of a candidate's behavior, focusing mainly on one's soft skills.

The premise of behavioral-based questions is that how one performed in the past is an accurate predictor of how one will perform in the future; thus, the more examples of how one performed particular skills should provide the interviewer(s) with an accurate assessment of the candidate's future performance. The rub against behavioral-based questions is that asking only one that addresses a particular skill is not enough to determine proficiency in that skill. So, if the interviewer(s) are trying to determine if the candidate is organized, one question based on organization is not enough. Three or even four will best determine if the candidate is proficient in that particular skill.

How do interviewers prepare for an interview that includes behavioral-based questions? Well, do you recall the competencies required of the job mentioned at the beginning of this chapter? There were 10 competencies mentioned in the job ad. Interviewers who prepare for an interview like this determine what skills they seek for their next hire, compose the job ad, and then create questions based on those skills. Perhaps the role they're trying to fill was occupied by someone who was strong in these skills, or perhaps the person previously lacked these particular skills. Perhaps this is a new role, and the employer wants to find the right person for it. An employer may have a "wish list" that is reflected in the preparation on the interviewer(s)' part. Consequently, an interview that includes behavioral-based questions can take a long time to conclude.

More than any type of question, the behavioral-based questions require intense preparation, which will be solace to the introvert who is strong at preparing for an interview. How do candidates prepare for interviews that include behavioral-based questions? The first step to prepare for these questions requires identifying the required competencies stated in the job ad, and then recalling specific times when you've performed each skill. In the case of the aforementioned job ad, it would require recalling 10 incidences when you performed the skills. The next step would be to write down a story about how you performed the skills. To introverts, this is a welcome moment to do their research and utilize their preference for writing.

The proper way to write the stories is to use the STAR (situation, task [your role in the situation], actions taken, and result(s)) formula. Some jobseekers prefer to see it as a PAR (problem, actions, result(s)) or CAR (challenge, actions, result(s)) formula. It matters not as long as you include all elements of the story. Write each piece of the story clearly, for example, the situation was…the task was…the actions were…the results were, and describe your STAR story in the same manner at the interview. How you designate the time to each element varies in some pundits' opinions, but a good structure to use can be: 20 percent to the beginning, 60 percent to the middle, and 20 percent to the end.

Where introverts can shine answering behavioral-based questions is by ensuring they've prepared stories that will cover the competencies asked for in the job ad. The stories must be specific, not broad, and to the point. Keep in mind that your story should not exceed two minutes and it should not veer from the topic at hand. So a more structured story, where you go as far as saying, "The situation was this…my task…my actions…the result was." In this way, the interviewer(s) understand you're telling a story to answer their question.

Why do stories work so well when answering behavioral-based questions? They work well because of the other skills they also reveal, not only the one requested from the interviewer(s). For example, the interviewers are determined to see if you are able to make changes that serve the customers. They say, "Tell us of a time when you had an idea to better serve the customers." You are prepared to answer this with a great example because you did your research on the job requirements.

"As the workshop facilitator," you begin, "I saw that some of our customers weren't being served as well as they could. We didn't have workshops to suit their needs (Situation). I took it upon myself to devise new, more challenging workshops (Your Task). What I did was first to query customers to see what they were looking for in our workshops. They told me more advanced workshops on CVs, interviewing, LinkedIn, networking, and others. With this information, I took the initiative to research, for example, CVs by calling employers and recruiters I knew to ask them what they look for in CVs. I took the information I accumulated and began the process of designing the CV workshop. This workshop and others took me about a week to complete (Actions). The end result was (1) my boss was delighted with my work and (2) the customers appreciated material that was more at their level.

A final word on interview questions. No good interview will be based entirely on traditional or behavioral-based questions. Traditional and situational questions are necessary to determine the candidates' job-related abilities, but aren't ideal in revealing candidates' personality skills, as they require answers that are theoretical. An interview that includes the appropriate combination of all types will be far more effective; thus, good interviewers conduct more challenging interviews that garner the most qualified candidates.

Concluding the interview

Do you have any questions for us?

It's funny how some people react to this question when I've asked them. Some looked at me with surprise, while others have asked me if they should have questions. My answer to the second question is, *definitely*. You must have questions to ask the interviewer(s) when they're done asking you questions. Why? In part because they want you to leave the interview with a better sense of what the job and company are about; but mostly because they want to see if you're serious about the position through the intelligent questions you ask them. Some agree that the questions you ask are nearly as important as the answers you provide to their questions.

This means that your questions have to be intelligent and not a waste of the interviewer(s) time. A question like, "What are the working hours?" shows no effort and, quite honestly, is irrelevant. Any questions related to salary and benefits are off limits until the company is willing to offer you the position. Your questions should focus on the position, company, and, if you're on top of the game, the competition. I advise my workshop attendees to write five questions on each of the aforementioned topics and bring their questions to the interview, written on paper or note cards. When asked if you have any questions, ask if you can refer to your questions. Very rarely will the interviewer(s) deny you this opportunity.

The questions you ask should also give you the opportunity to further promote your greatness. Think of a question like this: "What would you consider to be the greatest challenges of this job?" Their response might be: "Our customers tend to be extremely demanding and unaware of the technology, so the technical support personnel have their hands full."

Their answer is your open door, as you say: "Funny you should say that. We had a similar problem where I last worked. Many of our tech support did their best to answer our customers' technical questions, but got weary after a while and escalated the customers to me. I've always been very good at explaining complex technology at a level that many can understand. No, I don't see this as a problem."

The time you are given to ask questions should show your ability, as an introvert, to listen carefully to what was discussed during their questioning period. If you hear of a problem the company is having, this is your time to prolong the discussion of the problem if you are able to show your value in doing so. For example, the interviewer(s) said the company's efforts in social media have not been as strong as they should be. You may say, "Based on what you said earlier about your social media efforts, would you consider putting me on the social media campaign if I'm hired for this position? The reason I ask is because I have substantial experience in social media. I believe I could be of great assistance."

After you've asked your questions and the interviewers shake your hand—firmly but gently—your interview is not over. Next we're going to look at the thank you note.

The thank you note

The interview is not over until you send a unique thank you note to each person with whom you've interviewed. A lot of work? Definitely, but it's worth the effort if you want the position. Some rules about the thank you note:

> ➤ It must arrive with in 24 to 48 hours after the interview
>
> ➤ It can be written via e-mail, note card, or both
>
> ➤ It cannot be a form letter, a copy sent to each person who interviewed you
>
> ➤ It should not exceed one page

These are the basic rules. Why do you send a thank you note? You send a thank you note after an interview to show your gratitude to the people who took valuable time out of their schedule. Most likely they didn't enjoy the experience—no offense intended—but had to ask you tough questions to determine if you are the right person for the job.

You finished the most difficult part of the job search process; you made it through the verbal part of the process. Now, as an introvert, the thank you note is going to be easy. In the thank you note, you'll cover one or more of the following points of the interview:

> ➤ Touching upon something of interest said by one of the interviewers. Perhaps he or she made a comment about the job or company that you thought was intriguing. Now would be a good time to bring it up.
>
> ➤ Revisiting a question you didn't answer to your satisfaction. You've got nothing to lose, so why not elaborate on your answer?
>
> ➤ Offer a solution to a problem that was brought up in your discussions. In this case, you may want to write a short proposal about how you can help the company with its social media campaign, while also stating that this would be in addition to the job for which they're hiring you.

Summary

This chapter discussed many aspects of the interview, including how to act at an interview, the types of interviews you may face, the different types of questions, the importance of asking the interviewers questions, and the thank you note. But to be successful, you must first conduct research on the position and the company. This will better prepare you for the interview. Preparation for the interview entails more than doing your research; it means that everything is in order—your wardrobe, practicing answering questions you've written down, and participating in mock interviews. Preparation has been an important theme in this book so far, and will continue to play a major role in your success.

So what's next? In the next chapter, we'll look at some difficult questions you may face from the three types I discussed in this chapter: traditional, situational, and behavioral-based. I'll also tell you what the experts say about the challenges introverts may face answering these types of questions.

> 3

Some Difficult Questions You'll Face at the Interview

In the previous chapter, you learned about what steps you need to take before the interview and then how you must perform when you reach the coveted interview. You learned that research plays an integral role in your success. You also learned that you only have one chance to make a first impression with the interviewer(s), so don't blow it. There will be many types of interviews, not just one-on-ones, so you must prepare for any surprises. We also talked about three types of questions: traditional, situational, and behavioral-based questions. Behavioral-based questions will most likely be the most challenging for you, so we'll look at those very carefully in this chapter. Next we looked at the importance of closing the interview with questions of your own. Finally, we talked about the importance of the thank you note, the conclusion of the interview.

In this chapter, we'll look at the three types of questions and see how introverts should avoid revealing weaknesses and instead highlight their strengths. Are these questions necessarily meant to draw out introverts? Possibly—employers who are trying to fill positions that they feel are best suited for an extrovert (such as sales) may ask specific questions to determine if you're an introvert. Or they may ask certain questions that, unbeknownst to them, reveal your preference for introversion. They can be innocent questions that show your hand with the answers you give; therefore, it's important to think carefully about how you answer the three types of questions you may face at an interview.

Traditional questions

The traditional questions that follow may be asked to specifically determine if you're an introvert or extrovert, or may cause you to inadvertently reveal your preference. In some cases, there may be no consequences, while in other cases, the interviewer(s) may disqualify you for your preference. It is up to you to determine if the job is one that requires someone who is more extroverted or introverted. To play it safe, provide an honest answer that doesn't lean toward either dichotomy.

Tell me/us about yourself

On the surface, this directive doesn't seem difficult to answer, but there can be a snag in this otherwise innocent directive. Because this is very broad, it gives you the opportunity to describe your prior job-related experience and responsibilities. Simply avoid mentioning experience that paints you as a loner, for example, "I was responsible for many projects which I completed without supervision and assistance from other staff. I enjoyed this autonomy and satisfaction of completing the projects on my own." This answer would fit a job where independent work is required but not a job where teamwork is stressed. Emphasizing your written communication skills but avoiding talking about your verbal communications may, likewise, portray you as someone who has difficulty communicating with people.

The skill of two-way communication is very important to many companies, so be sure to talk about times when your verbal communication skills were also used in your work. Perhaps in addition to the responsibilities you handled with praise from your manager, you also worked across departments demonstrating great interpersonal skills. In today's work environment, every worker has to be able to work in collaboration with others.

Do you prefer working in groups or alone, and why?

Obviously the interviewer asks this question to determine if the candidates prefer the work performed by extroverts or introverts. An extrovert who is true to him/herself will answer that they prefer working in groups, whereas an introvert will say they prefer working alone. Many candidates will be tempted to answer that they can work in groups, as well as alone; but interviewers hear this answer far too often. The interviewer(s) want sincerity from the candidates, not canned answers.

The way to approach this question is by understanding what the job requires and if it's a match for your type. A sales position usually requires someone who likes working in groups and exchanging information. Though it's not out of the realm of possibility that you, as an introvert, would not find it exhausting to work in a group of extroverts, you'll have to convince the interviewer(s) that your preference is working in a group. Secretly, you'll think that some alone time will be just the thing for you when there's opportunity.

Positions like software engineer, accountant, market research analyst, graphic designer, and others, usually require someone who can work independently the majority of the time. (A Google search of jobs for introverts reveals many others, but the ones I've mentioned here are the most common.) Introverts naturally prefer to work independently but can also communicate with more extroverted types. You may want to add that although you like to work on your own, you are totally capable of interacting with project managers, sales people, upper management, and anyone else who needs your expertise.

How do you feel about working in an office, isolated from the rest of the team?

To this question you'll have to resist the urge to jump out of your chair and cheer for joy. This work setting is the opposite of an agile environment, where extroverts cherish constant verbal communications. The interviewer(s) may be trying to get a feel from you to see if you'll be happy working for the employer in this setting, or they may be testing your aversion to an open environment.

In either case, you don't want to come across as someone who is a loner who prefers to be holed up in an office and uncommunicative with the rest of the organization. This is a common perception of introverts—their inability to interact with other people in the organization—and perhaps why they're called shy or aloof.

In answering this question, be sure to state that working independently is fine as long as you have the opportunity to contribute to the teams within the organization. Provide an example of how you practice integration of services by lending your expertise to those who came to you with questions. Present yourself as adaptable, not inflexible.

As a manager, are you more hands on or hands off?

Most introverted managers are hands off. They prefer to delegate responsibility and be there for their subordinates whenever problems arise. Good managers are leaders who have a sense of what's working well and what's not. They know that some "observation" is necessary for flighty employees, while good employees need very little managing. One of my favorite managers told me that good managers don't manage. This was music to my ears.

If you answer "hands off" without any clarification, you may be perceived as someone who will have your door closed to all your employees (I've had one of these managers, as well). The proper response is that your success has come from empowering your employees, but when they required your guidance, you always had (literally) an open-door policy. You also checked in on their progress with appropriate frequency.

Most employees thrive when given a fair amount of autonomy, but some take advantage of the freedom. Be certain that you know the nature of your future employees. If they'll need constant babysitting, you'll have your work cut out for you. Introverts are not hand-holders.

You'll have to attend many tradeshows and entertain clients during the evenings. How do you feel about this?

Contrary to the question about working in an isolated or closed environment, this question may cause you to sink in your chair. This speaks to your ability to stand on your feet surrounded by boisterous people in a loud atmosphere and then catching a second wind to interact with people, most likely in a loud pub or restaurant. Introverts have the ability to adapt to work environments if they love what they do, but there is a price to pay for accepting work responsibilities that are contrary to your type. If this is work you'll love, save for the many tradeshows and nights out, it might be acceptable to you to endure the energy drain.

However, if you know your introverted side tells you that after a long day at a tradeshow you'd rather retire to your hotel room to read a novel, it may be time to thank the interviewer(s) for their time and look for a job that suits your introverted side more.

Tip

You could avoid this uncomfortable situation by knowing the nature of a position. This will require doing your research before accepting an invitation for an interview.

What do you do for fun?

This question is fairly harmless, as many similar activities are enjoyed by introverts and extroverts. What the interviewer(s) want to know is if you're the high-energy type or low-key type, or if you lead a sedentary life. At this time, your best answer is to choose neutral activities that introverts and extroverts both enjoy. I personally enjoy reading every night because it allows me to calm down, yet I also enjoy coaching football because I enjoy teaching children how to play the game properly. As well, I enjoy the occasional hike and a daily morning walk. Do I like going out every night to the pub or friends' houses? No, nor would I, or anyone in their right mind, say this at an interview.

Would you describe yourself as quiet or outgoing?

By now you should realize that this question is literally asking you if you're an introvert or extrovert and, to some extent, to see how much you know about the position. The job may require someone who is more reflective and independent, such as an accountant, engineer, or marketing communications writer. In this case, the proper person is someone who is "quiet." However, if the position requires someone who enjoys being around people around the clock, like a salesperson, event planner, or detective, the proper answer is "outgoing."

Some people would be inclined to say they're both outgoing and quiet in order to pass this answer, but remember that interviewers want an honest answer. You have an ultimate preference, so state it.

Do you speak up during meetings, or do you prefer to only speak occasionally?

This question sounds like it's coming from a frustrated manager who doesn't get enough input from the introverts in the group and gets too much inconsequential chatter from the extroverts. The truth of the matter is that introverts can hold their own at company meetings; they just take more time to formulate what they want to say. You may be a person who enjoys productive meetings without the useless banter from the extroverts. Say so, if this is the case.

If you proclaim that you dislike meetings altogether, this is a giveaway of your preference for introversion. Do you want to admit your preference? Probably not. Meetings are necessary for sharing information, building morale, and ultimately getting people on the same page. As mentioned earlier, there's a difference between productive and unproductive meetings. Explain how you've added to productive meetings by delivering important information and perhaps some levity when required.

How would you describe your relationship with your colleagues?

This question may raise a red flag. If you're speaking with an extroverted interviewer, your answer should include a mention of how you are very communicative with your colleagues on a professional level. If you're speaking with an interviewer who is an introvert, they'd understand your natural inclination to refrain from frivolous conversation. In this situation, you would benefit from being able to determine the introvert/extrovert preference of the interviewer.

This question is open-ended and may draw out more of the truth than you're willing to disclose. The best way to answer this is explain how you collaborate with your colleagues to get projects completed on time and under budget. Or you could talk about how you reach out to people in other departments in an effort to integrate services.

If you feel your colleagues respected you for your knowledge and insight, tell the interviewer this. Many colleagues have great relationships based on respect and professionalism, not necessarily camaraderie. So use words like, "collaborated," "trusted," and "respected."

We're a tight-knit group here, how do you feel about socializing after work?

This sort of question isn't always asked, but there may be some discussion of work-related socializing, so it is worth keeping in mind how you might respond.

When should you be completely truthful? Now. This question is telling of the company culture. Introverts generally prefer to retire to their home and enjoy a relaxing evening watching television with family and friends, or reading a great book. Don't present yourself as someone you're not. In other words, don't say, "That sounds great." You'll come across as disingenuous. Tell the interviewer(s) that while you enjoy a friendly work environment, you prefer to spend time with family and attend your kids' activities.

Here's where you need to draw a line in the sand. If this is the question that sinks your boat, this job was not meant for you. Let's say you're hired and management and your colleagues learn of your preference for being alone, rather than going out every night after work. They will see you as aloof, a non-team player. No one wants to be seen as that. Save yourself the trouble.

How important do you feel it is to listen to your customers?

This question is written for introverts, as listening is one of their greatest strengths. Talk about how one can't assist customers without understanding their needs. Tell the interviewer(s) that a great interaction is 80 percent listening and 20 percent persuasion. Emphasize that listening isn't only hearing the customers' words, it's reading their body language and hearing the words that aren't said. However, make certain that you don't give the interviewer(s) the impression that you're a sounding board who doesn't take action and close the deal.

What is your greatest weakness?

For some reason, this question is a job candidate's *greatest* fear. Whether you're an introvert or extrovert, the answer should never be about personality skills, for example perfectionism, hardworking—yes, some say working hard is their greatest weakness—impatience, and so on. Instead, choose a skill that is something correctable, like a technical skill. Let me give you an example. You're applying for a project manager's position which you know—based on your research of the position—will involve presenting to large groups. *Don't* say speaking in front of people makes you uncomfortable. Even though you'll come across as honest, this is a weakness that is difficult (although not impossible) to overcome. Telling the interviewer(s) your weakness is creating PowerPoint presentations is more acceptable, as well as honest. Don't end your answer at that. Say you've trained yourself to become proficient in MS Word and Excel, so learning PowerPoint will take no more than one or two weeks at most. Besides, there's usually a PowerPoint guru who would love to create your PowerPoint presentations.

Next we'll look at situational questions, which are asked by interviewers to determine how well you know the position for which you're applying. These questions tend to be more difficult to answer than the traditional question, though. But like the traditional questions, situational questions only require theoretical answers or speculative responses. The behavioral-based questions are the most difficult of the three, as they demand specific occasions when you've demonstrated the skills required by the employer.

Situational questions

Situational questions are challenging for job candidates because they test their knowledge of the position. Anyone who hasn't done their research will do poorly in answering these questions. In my mind, these questions are more difficult than the traditional questions, as they ask you to put yourself in the shoes of someone who is performing the task to the satisfaction of the interviewer(s). Nonetheless, these questions require a theoretical or hypothetical answer. Situational questions begin with an opening like this, "What would you do in this situation?" or "Given this situation, how would you react?"

If you came across two of your subordinates arguing, how would you handle the situation?

In her book, *The Introvert Advantage: How to Thrive in an Extrovert World*, Marti Olsen Laney, Psy.D., writes:

> *"While some people, usually extroverts, thrive on seeing the sparks fly; other people, usually introverts, are conflict adverse. They'll do anything rather than face a fight. Conflicts take up their energy, and they go out of their way to avoid them."*

This question not only tests introverts' decision-making abilities, it determines how they deal with conflict—if they deal with conflict at all. The ability to deal with conflict is part of being a manager or supervisor, albeit not a desirable part, along with the many responsibilities they perform.

As Olsen Laney asserts, introverts aren't comfortable with dealing with conflict. It consumes too much of their energy. Introverts generally prefer written communications over verbal communications, but in a situation where two employees are arguing, there's no time to sit down and write an action statement. The time is now, and action must be taken on the spot.

On the other hand, your answer should not indicate rash behavior on your part. Extroverts, who are quicker to act than think, may say how they'd handle the situation on the spot, drawing attention to the conflict. The proper way to handle a situation like this would be to separate the two combatants, bring one and then the other into a separate room to hear their side of the story, and finally meet with both of them in the room to mediate the situation. Introverts tend to think before acting. Don't indicate that you would overthink the situation.

Because this question, like most traditional and situational questions, can be rehearsed, you should have a strong answer in mind before entering the interview. This question, or a question similar to it, will most likely be asked if you are applying for a leadership role.

You suggest an idea for a project that your boss doesn't agree with. What would you do?

This question can pose quite a challenge to anyone who is leery of conflict, and this situation hints toward a conflict between the candidate and the boss. It's also believed by many pundits that introverts generally require more time than extroverts to process information and develop a cohesive response. A confrontation like this scenario, especially with a superior, is added pressure that introverts can do without.

The good news is that confrontation with a superior is unnecessary if this situation is handled a different way. As the introverted candidate, you realize that proof is the best way to convince a supervisor; your supervisor doesn't want to argue the point either. Proof of your point will be the winning approach to this situation; therefore, your first step is to gracefully recede from the possible conflict. Devising a well-thought out idea or prototype, the proof, is your second step. Finally, presenting your boss with your tangible idea is the final and winning step. Confrontation is avoided.

What would you do if you were given two assignments by two managers of equal status, both of whom supervise you?

The clear solution to this is establishing communication between the two managers, but introverts may consider doing this a difficult task if verbal communication must be established. Your natural response to this question may be to explain that you'd send an e-mail addressed to both managers explaining the conflict. And this might work; but does the interviewer(s) want someone who will be more assertive, someone who will address both managers, possibly bringing them together in the same room? You bet they do. Direct verbal communication is the quickest, most effective way to handle a conundrum like this.

When delivering your rehearsed answer, be sure to sound convincing. You can improve communications between the two managers who have their own agendas by respectfully asking them if you can have a minute to discuss the two assignments you've been given. Say you would ask them to prioritize the two assignments. Given this request, most reasonable managers would come to a conclusion as to which assignment requires top priority.

One twist to this situation is when the two managers are not in the same location, separated by the Atlantic Ocean. In this case, your response to this answer is that you'll grab the manager in your business and suggest that the two of you get on a conference call with the other manager. Problem averted.

This position requires the ability to speak with clients at various functions. How will you handle this?

Small talk alert. At the interview is not the time to plan the topics you'll discuss with a client; this is too late. Based on your knowledge of the position, the company, and the company's client, you'll be better prepared to answer this question. You may supply a general answer to this question, but knowing the aforementioned facts will serve you best. Understanding the client's needs regarding the company's products or services will be a major part of conversation. This is when you can exercise one of your greatest attributes as an introvert, your listening skills. Correct. Tell the interviewer(s) you'll ask questions to get a better idea of the client's needs, because only when you know the needs of the client will you be able to address them.

Explain to the interviewer(s) what you know about the company's products or services and then tell them you'll use this information to add more depth to the discussion with the client. As I've mentioned before, the introverts' ability to research is one of their many strengths. Unlike extroverts, introverts are usually not as quick at coming up with spontaneous dialog. But the content of the introverts' discussion is usually more in depth and thoughtful. More banter and quick remarks are not necessarily better in this case.

Tell me the steps you would take in preparing a presentation for a large audience

Introverts are as capable of delivering presentations as extroverts are—it's the volume of presentations that pose a problem for introverts. I'm an introvert and I've delivered thousands of presentations. Many introverts—me included—have been accused of being an extrovert because of their enthusiasm for the topic, which speaks to the verbal communication skills introverts possess. Do you think introverts don't practice their public speaking skills? Of course they do. It's generally believed that introverts require more preparation than extroverts do, as they need to process what they're going to present to a large group of people. Once they are prepared to deliver their topic, introverts are just as capable as extroverts are at wowing a crowd.

You must be able to explain your presentation experience and skills, while stressing how you prepare for public speaking. Don't come across as a perfectionist, however. Employers want to know that you can also think on your feet, and that you won't be ruffled by any problems that may arise. I know that if the room assignment has been changed to a room with which I'm unfamiliar, I'll be fine. A small inconvenience will not defeat me.

You'll prepare by first understanding your audience. Are they highly technical like engineers and project managers, or are they less technical like sales people? Second is doing your research on the topic. Next you'll talk about the platform you'll use, whether it's PowerPoint, Prezi, or a simple flip chart. Finally, you'll tell the interviewer(s) how you use all forms of communications—verbal, body language, and listening to your audience —to succeed at an interview.

We've looked at traditional and situational questions, examining the challenges both types of questions present to introverts. Next, we'll look at behavioral-based questions, which are more challenging than the traditional and situational questions. You'll understand why your ability to prepare for an interview that entails behavioral-based questions is essential to succeed at one of the most successful interviews, from the employers' point of view.

Behavioral-based questions

When it comes to behavioral-based interviews, Armando Llorente, SPHR and VP of Human Resources at Clark & Lavey, a consulting firm in New Hampshire, USA, knows a thing or two about interviewing candidates. He's interviewed hundreds of candidates for various positions at Fortune 500 companies. He says this about the behavioral-based interviewing style:

> *"Recruiters and hiring managers often use behavioral-based interview questions to elicit short-story responses from a candidate. The answer expected involves a recap by the candidate of how he demonstrated a particular competency or qualification important to the job. For example, for a customer service position, the recruiter asks the individual to provide an example where he dealt with an irate customer and what he did to resolve their issue(s.) Another example, for an engineering job, a candidate is asked to describe a situation where he/she was asked to 'debug' a malfunctioning machine tool and use all the necessary engineering technicians to fix the problem."*

Behavioral-based questions are in fact directives because they begin with "Tell me about a time when..." or, "Give me an example of when..." To answer them successfully, you must employ the STAR formula (**S**ituation, **T**ask, **A**ctions, **R**esult(s)); although, the PAR (**P**roblem, **A**ctions, **R**esult(s)) or CAR (**C**hallenge, **A**ctions, **R**esults) formulas can work as well. The preferred ratio of the aforementioned components is 20 percent situation/task, 60 percent actions, and 20 percent results; although this is not a steadfast rule.

Let's look at some behavioral-based questions that might be difficult for introverts to answer.

Tell me about the most important project you worked on

This question addresses how job candidates approach the project, their task in the project, the actions they took, and the final result(s). If you worked on a team, the interviewer(s) want to know how extensive your role in the team was; in what manner you collaborated with your team members; if you pulled your weight; and if the project was completed on time, under budget, and how much revenue it generated.

Here's where I see how introverts can answer this question successfully or fail in their delivery. First, did you contribute to the chemistry of the team? Were you an active member, or did you retreat to your cubicle or office to complete your task? This speaks to your ability to communicate with your team members, a concern some interviewers may have about their next hire. They want to know that they will be a proactive team lead, not someone who will sit in their office with the door shut. Let's look at how a team lead on a data storage software project may answer this question by indicating the interaction they had with their team members:

> ➤ **Situation**: We had to develop a product that would be compatible with multi-tiered jukeboxes in the largest hospital in Boston.

> ➤ **Task**: As the team leader, I had to make sure engineering and technical support would have the product ready to ship by a tight deadline, approximately 2 months.

> ➤ **Action**: So I held an initial meeting to get the three engineers and four tech support people on the same page. Engineering would be responsible for delivering revisions to tech support for any bugs along the way.

> ➤ **Action**: I required weekly reports on the progress of the product. If we were behind our schedule, I would request that my team put in extra work after work hours, and some of them came into work with me during the weekends. (Smile)

> ➤ **Action**: The team and I determined that we would communicate via e-mail whenever possible, as daily meetings would be time-consuming. (An extrovert interviewer may see through the introvert candidate on this one.)

> ➤ **Action**: One of my largest roles was to create the manual that would be edited by our hardworking technical writer and later serve as some marketing literature—I created descriptions of the product.

> ➤ **Action**: The president of the company wanted to be updated as to the progress of the product, so I would meet with him bi-weekly for very short meetings. He was very pleased with the progress of the team and often sent e-mails of praise to each member of the team.

> ➤ **Positive, quantified result with a little cherry on top**: I'm very happy to say that the product shipped a week before the deadline and, most importantly, it was bug free. My team was acknowledged at an impromptu company party for our outstanding work, and our customer wrote a letter to the CEO saying they had implemented our software and it was working better than they expected.

Tip

Another rule to abide by is keeping your answers to less than two minutes. This answer would be a minute and a half. For answers that describe a time you didn't succeed, these should be as short as possible.

Now that you know how to structure an answer to a behavioral-based question, let's look at some other questions that can be challenging for introverts, or anyone for that matter.

Tell us about a time when you strained a relationship and what you did about it

The interviewer(s) ask this question to determine how well you can bounce back from a mistake and, in particular, use your verbal communications skills to accomplish it. The interviewer(s) may inquire about a relationship you strained with a colleague or customer or boss. The key part of this question is not about how you strained a relationship. In fact, this part of your answer should be brief. The most important component of your answer is what you did about your mistake, and the actions you took. This is where you'll elaborate on your ability to mend fences.

Where introverts may fall down in the mending fence phase is their discomfort in reaching out to talk to the customer, partner, media, or whomever they offended. This could be a weak point, unless you're one who can get beyond your comfort zone and make the phone call(s) or meet with the offended party. This question also speaks to the introverts' aversion to conflict, which Olsen Laney says takes up a great deal of energy. You cannot come across as someone who is unwilling or incapable of taking the steps to fix the strained relationships.

Because this is a question that will reveal your vulnerability, make your answer brief with a possible happy ending. I remember when I was in marketing and I published a product release in the newsletter I wrote. When I called an editor of a local trade magazine to brag about our new product, she said it was too late to publish the news in her magazine. I had let the proverbial cat out of the bag.

I learned a hard lesson through my faux pas, so the next time the company released a product, I called the editor first with the good news. She not only published the news in her magazine, she highlighted the release at the beginning of the magazine.

What did you learn?

I was successful in mending the fence and I learned that I shouldn't jump too quickly—there is protocol in public relations.

Tell me about a time when you persuaded your boss to accept an idea of yours

Do you remember a version of this from the situational questions? Think about how much more difficult it is to come up with an actual time when you performed the skill of persuasion. You can't give a theoretical response; you must give a specific occasion when you demonstrated your ability to persuade a person of higher authority. Maybe it was a time when you tried to persuade your dispassionate boss to adopt a social media campaign, which you wanted to spearhead.

And in this case you didn't stand there for hours going toe-to-toe with your higher authority; rather you retreated to your cubicle and gathered information to support your assertions. In fact, you gathered URLs for your main competitors that showed their Twitter, Facebook, and LinkedIn buttons. "If they're doing it, why aren't we?" was your unspoken message. Then you found an article from a reputable publication that said social media increases B2C sales by 40 percent. If that weren't enough, you found a personal statement from the president of your **major** competitor exclaiming that their social media campaign is a major reason for territory growth.

Now you were ready to go to your boss with the firepower you needed to persuade him to let you take on the social media campaign. "OK," your boss agreed with a smirk, "but you can't let any of your responsibilities slack." No problem, you thought. And you smiled on the way out the door because of your small victory.

Give me an example of when you were able to adapt to different managers/ supervisors.

Daniel Pink is not the only person to describe ambiversion. In his book *To Sell is Human: The Surprising Truth About Moving Others*, he writes:

> *"Most of us aren't on the extremes— uniformly extrovert or rigidly introvert. We're in the middle— and that allows us to move up and down the curve, attuning ourselves as circumstances demand, and discovering the hidden powers of ambiversion."*

This is one way to look at introverts' ability to adapt to different circumstances, or in this case, managers. After all, we are able to utilize all traits on the introversion/extroversion continuum. Those who are nearest to either introversion or extroversion will have an easier time of adapting to any situation. There are generally two types of managers: those who are hands off and those who are hands on. Most introverts would prefer managers who leave them alone to do their work, not managers who are constantly calling them into their office or popping their head into the introverts' office.

Chances are you've had both types of managers. I know I have. I recall in my marketing days when I had a manager who would stay in her office and call me or send an e-mail only when she needed to run something by me. I would go days between conversations, and I liked that.

Then I took a job at another company where my manager was very hands-on—does the word "micromanage" come to mind? It took some adjusting, but I knew she was so invested in the success of our marketing department that she wanted to know on a minute basis how things were going. It didn't take long before I came to grips with this and actually felt as relaxed as I did with my hands-off manager. "What's up, boss?" I would say to her as she poked her head in my door. Ambiversion is not acknowledged by the **Myers-Briggs Type Indicator (MBTI)**. You're either an introvert or an extrovert, but what Pink refers to is someone who can adapt to any situation. What a fine state of mind to be in.

Tell us about a time when you made a sale despite the objections of the customer

To answer this question, the job candidate would probably pose a response similar to what Pink is describing in the ambivert. The successful salesperson is someone who, like an introvert, has the ability to listen and, like an extrovert, has the ability to close the sale with persuasive dialog when the time is right.

One night I was talking to a District Manager of Sales as we were driving to a basketball game. I was curious what he'd say if I asked him what he considers to be the most important trait of a great salesperson. His answer, without hesitation, was persistence. And then he said the second trait is listening skills. Bingo. *One of the best traits of an introvert.* I then asked him about the ability to talk to the customer. He said listening is still more important and then went on to recount a time when he was on a conference call with one of his salesmen who "wouldn't shut up long enough to listen to the customer." It was at that moment when I wondered whether my traveling companion, who was a very successful District Manager of Sales, was an extrovert or introvert…or perhaps an ambivert.

In telling your story, be sure you emphasize how you listened to the customer's needs, considering all possible objections and how you would meet those objections, how you carefully thought about what you'd say to your customer, and finally how you closed the sale by hitting the customer's hot spots. Introverts and extroverts can come across as one-dimensional if they fail to talk about the strengths of both types, listening and speaking. Don't cast yourself as someone who can only listen and not act upon the information you've accumulated.

One more thing

"Introverts who haven't thought a lot about their own personal mottos, what they stand for, what's important to them in the character arena; may take too much time to answer a question and be concerned afterward that they didn't answer it correctly."

–Julee Wingo, Learning and Development Specialist at Kellogg Company

If it isn't enough that introverts may be challenged by a plethora of interview questions, this statement indicates that the pressure to answer the questions, whether traditional or behavioral-based, is amplified if the candidate isn't prepared. Preparation is a word that I and other job-search experts throw around like a handful of pebbles, which isn't to say we're not serious. Being prepared means you've done your research—one of your major strengths—on the position and company, as well as the competition. Being prepared may allow you to anticipate what questions will be asked at the interview. Knowing, generally speaking, what questions will be asked puts you in a better position to succeed at the interview.

Always keep in mind that you, an introverted job candidate, are as capable of doing as well at the interview as your counterpart, the extrovert. You are qualified to do the job because you were vetted by HR, the recruiter, and the hiring manager. Now it's time to show them through your interviewing skills that you are a sure bet.

Summary

In this chapter, we looked at the three types of interview questions and how some of them can pose a problem for introverts. Certainly there are questions that stump extroverts, but because the interview is an arena where verbal skills are needed most, extroverts are given a head start. Some believe that the pressure of the interview troubles introverts, not only the questions. Therefore, being prepared for the interview is essential for success. Prepare for every interview like it's the light at the end of the tunnel. Go to interviews for your dream jobs. Go to interviews even if you're not sure you'll want the job. Go to interviews for practice. No one will tell the employer you're wasting his time, especially me. Don't go to an interview if you're unprepared.

First take some time to learn more about your preference for introversion by taking the Myers-Briggs Type Indicator. Your local career center may administer it free of charge. Talk with other introverts to learn how they think. Talk to extroverts to learn how they think. The more you understand about your strengths and challenges, the better perspective you'll have on the job search.

Remember that there are various types of interviews, not just one-on-one interviews. Mentally prepare yourself for group, situational, and telephone interviews, as well as interviews that are poorly conducted—usually by hiring managers. Don't get caught off guard. Once at the interview, make eye contact, deliver a firm but gentle handshake, and engage in small talk with the interviewer(s). Most importantly, be prepared to answer the tough questions. We've looked at a fraction of tough questions interviewers will ask—interviewers are constantly coming up with trickier questions as they try to find candidates who will pass their tests.

The word "preparation" is probably the most important word in the job-search process, so make this your top priority. Allow me to leave you with a quote:

Before anything else, preparation is the key to success.

–Alexander Graham Bell